Running through this little book on the Reformation
is the surprising legacy of joy. The fact that we have
no portraits of any Reformers smiling is a fluke of history.
Nobody smiled for portraits until fifty years ago! If you want
to know what made this movement explosively joyful,
don't look at the pictures, read this book.

JOHN PIPER

Founder and teacher, desiringGod.org;
Chancellor, Bethlehem College & Seminary, Minneapolis, Minnesota

As I read this thrilling little introduction to the Reformation
my heart started to beat with joy. For this 500th anniversary
I'm going to try to persuade everyone to read it.

RICO TICE

Senior Minister at All Souls Church, Langham Place

KT-482-595

Thank God for the world changing Reformation recovering the truth of the all sufficient cross of Christ! As Michael Reeves points out in his inspiring text, prior to the Reformation religion was disguising the problem rather than solving it. Five hundred years later people from around the world with open Bibles celebrate the rediscovery of light that dispelled their overwhelming darkness.

TERRY VIRGO

Founder of NewFrontiers,
an international network of over 1,500 churches

Immensely readable. In these few pages not only is Martin Luther brought to life but the rediscovery of a world changing message for all centuries in all its relevance for today is given wings.

TREVOR ARCHER

FIEC London Director

Captivating and heart-warming vignettes of the (now famous) freedom-fighters whose radical discovery re-shaped Western Europe and impacted the world. Their story is beautifully captured in this charming little book.

RICHARD CUNNINGHAM

Director of UCCF: the Christian Unions

FREEDOM MOVEMENT

500 YEARS OF REFORMATION

MICHAEL REEVES

FOR

What did the reformation ever do

FIVE HUNDRED YEARS AGO A DISCOVERY WAS MADE THAT WOULD CHANGE THE WORLD, UNLEASHING HAPPINESS WHEREVER IT WENT.

Still today it is transforming
lives and cultures.

The secret was this: failing, broken people 'are not loved because they are attractive,' said Martin Luther, 'they are attractive because they are loved.'

That could not be more countercultural. It is deep in our blood today that the more attractive we make ourselves, the more loved and happy we will be. The Reformation is the story of one man discovering to his delight that with God, it is the other way round. God does not love people because they have sorted themselves out: he loves failures. And that love makes them flourish.

It started on 31 October 1517, when Martin Luther, a German monk, posted ninety-five theses for debate on the door of the Castle Church in Wittenberg. The theses were about matters of love and forgiveness, but the reason he wrote them, he explained, was because if these matters were not dealt with, it would 'make Christians unhappy'.

Martin Luther was concerned with people's happiness. In fact, he would come to believe that he had found the secret of happiness. And that, at its heart, was what the Reformation was all about. Not moralizing. Not self-improvement. It was a discovery of stunningly happy news – news that would transform millions of lives and change the world.

This is the story of that discovery.

From despair to

DELI

CHAPTER 2

THE TWENTY-ONE-YEAR-OLD SCREAMED

Caught in a sudden and violent storm while walking to his university in Erfurt, Germany, a lightning bolt smashed him to the ground. Terrified, he cried out 'Saint Anne, help me! I shall become a monk!'

The young Martin Luther survived, he upheld his vow and began a monastic life.

In a sense he loved it. Luther's deepest fear was of dying and having to stand before God his Judge. But becoming a monk gave him what he saw as a golden opportunity: he could make himself more attractive to God and so – hopefully – earn his love.

And he went for it. Every few hours he would leave his tiny monastery cell and make his way to a service in the chapel, starting with matins in the middle of the night, then another at six in the morning, another at nine, another at twelve, and

so on. He often took no bread or water for three days at a time, and was quite prepared deliberately to freeze himself in the winter cold in the hope that he might please God. Driven to confession, he would exhaust his confessors, taking up to six hours at a time to catalogue his most recent sins.

Yet the more he did, the more troubled he became. Was it enough? Were his motives right? Luther found himself sinking into an ever-deeper introspection.

He began to sense that his moral dirtiness and lack of attractiveness to God went deeper than his behaviour. He came to see

himself as a man curved in on himself and fundamentally selfish. All his good conduct and religious behaviour was only disguising the problem, not solving it.

Worse, he was coming to see God as a loveless tyrant who demands perfection and gives nothing but punishment. 'Though I lived as a monk without reproach, I felt that I was a sinner before God with an extremely disturbed conscience,' he later wrote. 'I did not love, yes, I hated the righteous God who punishes sinners, and secretly, if not blasphemously, certainly murmuring greatly, I was angry with God.'

And in that dark, dark place he made his happy discovery.

Studying the Bible in his cell, he was struggling to understand what the apostle Paul meant in his letter to the Romans:

'For in the gospel the righteousness of God is revealed – a righteousness that is by faith from first to last, just as it is written: "The righteous will live by faith."'

Romans 1:17

What on earth could that mean? And what exactly is 'the righteousness of God'?

Is it that God is perfect and I'm not? So I can't be with him? That's what Luther had thought. But 'I began to understand that the righteousness of God is that by which the righteous person lives: by a gift of God.'

HERE IN THE BIBLE, LUTHER FOUND, TRULY IS GOOD NEWS: A KIND AND GENEROUS GOD... WHO LOVES FIRST.

It was as if his whole world had flipped inside out. God, he saw, is not asking us to earn his love and acceptance in any way. God's righteousness is something he shares with us as a gift. Acceptance before God, forgiveness and peace with him is received by simple faith or trust.

Here in the Bible, Luther found, truly is good news: a kind and generous God who does not ask people to make themselves attractive before he loves them, but who loves first.

Instead of trusting in his own efforts to be good, Luther saw simply that he could accept God's word of promise. Then all his struggles and all his anxiety could be replaced with happy confidence and peace.

'Here,' said Luther ecstatically, 'I felt that I was altogether born again and had entered paradise itself through open gates.'

LUTHER AT HOME

Martin Luther was no stained-glass saint.

Red-blooded, beer-swilling, and often rude, he was proof of his own discovery – that God's love and forgiveness are for real imperfect people. Take his marriage to a runaway nun.

As his message of good news got out, many monks and nuns wanted to join him in leaving the monastic life. He even helped one group of nuns escape. On Easter morning 1523, he sent a herring merchant to their convent with a covered wagon full of empty herring barrels. Nine nuns were smuggled out to a new life in Wittenberg.

Two years later, he was married to one of them: Katie von Bora. And clearly Martin and Katie enjoyed each other's company, whether walking with their dog in the garden, fishing together or eating with friends. Martin had a bowling alley built in the garden for when he broke from his work, while Katie looked after the household (and its private brewery).

Twice, however, tragedy struck. Martin and Katie had five children, but both daughters died young – one of them, Magdelene, in her father's arms. Martin wept over her coffin, yet his discovery gave him

the confidence to declare 'She will rise again at the last day.'

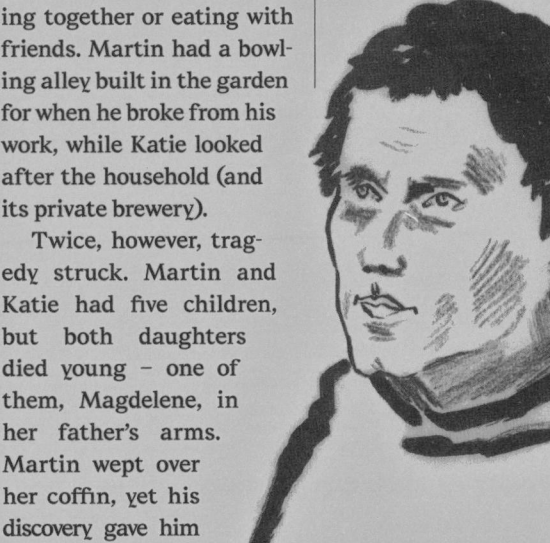

The joyful

EXCHANGE

CHAPTER 3

LUTHER SOON WROTE A LITTLE BOOKLET TO EXPLAIN HIS DISCOVERY.

He called it
The Freedom of a Christian.

In it he said that the good news he had found was like the story of a wealthy king (representing Jesus Christ) who marries a debt-ridden prostitute (representing someone who will trust him).

The girl could never make herself a queen. But then the king comes along, full of love for her. And on their wedding day he makes his marriage vow to her. With that she is his, and the prostitute becomes a queen. He takes and bears all her debts, and she now shares his boundless wealth and royal status.

It is not that she earned it. She didn't become a queen by behaving royally. Indeed, she does not know how to behave royally. But when the king made his marriage promise, he changed her status. For all her backstreet ways, the prostitute is now a queen.

Just so, found Luther, the greatest failure who accepts Jesus Christ gets to share his righteousness and status. What happens is a happy status-swap: when Jesus died on the cross, he took and there dealt with all our guilt and failure; and out of sheer love he now shares with those who'll trust him all his righteousness and life.

Jesus Christ's death on the cross was the key moment for what Luther called 'the joyful exchange'. On the cross Jesus, who wasn't guilty, took and faced God's punishment for our guilt so that we could be forgiven.

'There was no remedy except for God's only Son to step into our distress', he wrote. But because of the cross, 'God is reconciled thereby and receives into grace and forgiveness of sins all who believe in this Son.'

Jesus loves broken people and through his death on the cross for them, makes them attractive and beautiful in God's sight.

It means, wrote Luther happily, 'Her sins cannot now destroy her, since they are laid upon Christ and swallowed up by him. And she has that righteousness in Christ, her husband, which she may boast of as her own and say, "If I have sinned, yet my Christ, in whom I believe, has not sinned, and all his is mine and all mine is his."'

'MY CHAINS FELL OFF'

One of the great literary classics to flow out of the Reformation was John Bunyan's *Pilgrim's Progress*.

A metalworker by trade, Bunyan travelled from village to village with a 60lb anvil and hefty toolkit on his back: it became a model for the great burden of guilt his Pilgrim carries on his back (until he comes to the cross and it is 'loosed from off his shoulders' to his enormous relief).

In his youth, Bunyan had been much like Martin Luther: driven to despair by his guilt, fearing 'Christ would not forgive me.' Then he made the exact same discovery as Luther:

'But one day, as I was passing in the field, and that too with some stains on my conscience, fearing lest yet all was not right, suddenly this sentence fell upon my soul, Thy righteousness is in heaven; and I saw, with the eyes of my soul, Jesus Christ at God's right hand; there, I say, is my righteousness; so that wherever I was, or whatever I was a-doing, God could not say of me, He wants my righteousness, for that was just before Him.'

He saw, in other words, that it was not how good about himself he felt that mattered. Feeling good or feeling bad, 'my righteousness was Jesus Christ Himself, the same yesterday, and to-day, and for ever. Now did my chains fall off my legs indeed, I was loosed from my affliction and irons ... now went I also home rejoicing, for the grace and love of God.'

FIRST EDITION COVER
Pilgrim's Progress is one of the most published books in the English language. Bunyan wrote it while he was in prison for preaching.

JUST A CLEAN-UP?

People sometimes think of the Reformation
as little more than a five-hundred-year-old
clean-up job on the Roman Catholic Church,
which is quite misleading.

Certainly things had got a bit grubby before the Reformation. Rome – which had become the Las Vegas of its day – had just reached an all-time low under the papacy of Pope Alexander VI (1492–1503). Having bought the necessary votes to get himself elected, he proceeded to have numerous children by his mistresses, he was rumoured to have had another with his party-throwing, poison-ring wearing daughter Lucrezia, and is best remembered for his habit of throwing orgies in the Vatican and poisoning his cardinals.

Yet it was others, not Luther, who dedicated themselves to opposing such moral corruption. Almost everyone seemed eager for that sort of reform. In Florence, thousands thronged to hear Girolamo Savonarola's sermons condemning Pope Alexander VI. Everyone laughed when the poet Dante placed Popes Nicholas III and Boniface VIII in the eighth circle of hell in his Divine Comedy. Of course there were corrupt old popes and priests who drank too much before Mass.

But.

If that had been what Luther was about, he'd have been forgotten in a decade.

Five hundred years on, we remember the Reformation because it was not just another call to do better. It was the recovery of a message that had got buried – a world-changing message good for all centuries.

Martin Luther had stumbled across something people had not heard of in their day: 'sinners are attractive because they are loved; they are not loved because they are attractive.'

Now you're
speaking my

LANG

UAGE!

CHAPTER 4

LUTHER HAD MADE HIS DISCOVERY THROUGH READING THE BIBLE. BUT FEW OTHERS HAD ACCESS TO A BIBLE, OR COULD READ IT.

In the years that followed he therefore set about translating the Bible into an easy, everyday German so that all around him 'might seize and taste the clear, pure Word of God.'

Soon others were making the same happy discovery in the Bible. In England, a young priest called Thomas Bilney read it and come across the words 'Christ Jesus came into the world to save sinners'. Previously he had been consumed with guilt, but with these words, he said,

'Immediately I seemed unto myself inwardly to feel a marvellous comfort and quietness, insomuch that my bruised bones leaped for joy. After this, the Scripture began to be more pleasant unto me than the honey or the honey-comb.'

To be so excited about the Bible strikes most today as odd. But the message people were finding there – that God lavishes his love and forgiveness not on the deserving but on all who'll trust him – was like a burst of Mediterranean sunshine into a grey world of guilt and shame.

Another Englishman who made the same find – a brilliant young linguist named William Tyndale – described the discovery as

'... good, merry, glad and joyful tidings, that maketh a man's heart glad and maketh him sing, dance, and leap for joy.'

SO GREAT WAS THE EXCITEMENT THAT PRIESTS COMPLAINED OF HOW, EVEN DURING THE SERMON, LAYPEOPLE WERE READING THE BIBLE ALOUD TO EACH OTHER.

Wanting others to read what he had read and so share his joy, Tyndale set about his life's work of translating the Bible from its original Greek and Hebrew into English.

He sailed to Germany, where it was safer to work. And there, within a few short years, Tyndale managed to translate most of the Bible. Accurate and easy to read, it turned out to be a gem of a translation. However, it was illegal in England to own or even read such a translation – and the penalty was death.

Some 16,000 copies of his Bible were smuggled into England before he was caught in 1535. The following October he was officially strangled and burned near Brussels, uttering the immortal last words 'Lord, open the King of England's eyes!'

Just two years after Tyndale had died uttering that prayer, it was decreed by the king that an English bible be placed in every church in England. King Henry VIII ordered 'ye shall discourage no man from the reading or hearing of the Bible, but shall expressly provoke, stir and exhort every person to read the same as that which is the very lively word of God.'

Six English bibles were placed in St Paul's Cathedral, crowds immediately thronging round those who could read loud enough to make themselves heard. So great was the excitement that priests complained of how, even during the sermon, laypeople were reading the Bible aloud to each other.

The message – and the excitement – were spreading.

THE REFORMATION'S ODE TO JOY

by Martin Luther,
trans. Frederic Henry Hedge.

A mighty fortress is our God,
A bulwark never failing;
Our shelter He, amid the flood
Of mortal ills prevailing.
For still our ancient foe
Doth seek to work us woe;
His craft and pow'r are great,
And, armed with cruel hate,
On earth is not his equal.

Did we in our own strength confide,
Our striving would be losing;
Were not the right Man on our side,
The Man of God's own choosing.
Dost ask who that may be?
Christ Jesus, it is He;
Lord Sabaoth His name,
From age to age the same,
And He must win the battle.

And tho' this world, with devils filled,
Should threaten to undo us;
We will not fear, for God hath willed
His truth to triumph through us.
The prince of darkness grim –
We tremble not for him;
His rage we can endure,
For lo! his doom is sure,
One little word shall fell him.

That word above all earthly pow'rs –
No thanks to them – abideth:
The Spirit and the gifts are ours
Thro' Him who with us sideth.
Let goods and kindred go,
This mortal life also;
The body they may kill:
God's truth abideth still,
His kingdom is forever.

The
sweetest

PLEA

SURE

CHAPTER 5

'MAN'S CHIEF END [POINT] IS TO GLORIFY GOD, AND TO ENJOY HIM FOREVER.'

Those words, written by a team of scholars in Westminster in the 1640s, capture the heart of the Reformation.

For what Luther's discovery had made abundantly clear was that God is glorious: beautiful, good, kind and generous. We can therefore actually enjoy God. Not hate. Not avoid. Enjoy.

The practical consequences throughout cultures influenced by the Reformation were vast. Take Johann Sebastian Bach, an ardent Lutheran all the way down to his tapping toes. When satisfied with his musical compositions, Bach would write on them 'S. D. G.' for Soli Deo Gloria ('Glory to God Alone'). For through his music he wanted to sound out the beauty and glory of God, so pleasing both God and people.

The glory of God, he believed, gratuitously rings out through sunsets, stars, mountain peaks and music, bringing joy wherever it is appreciated. And the enjoyment of those things can give people a taste of how enjoyable is their Creator.

God, Bach saw, is to be enjoyed. In fact, the deepest and most satisfying happiness can only be found in knowing God.

This was all quite different to what so many had known before. As a monk, Luther had said, 'I did not love, yes, I hated the righteous God.' Doubtful of whether they had made themselves worthy of heaven, people shook with fear at the thought of how God might judge them.

You can still feel it when you see a medieval fresco of the Last Judgment, the naked dead seized by grotesque demons and forced into the fire. You can hear it in the words of the Dies Irae that would be chanted in every Mass for the Dead:

'Day of wrath, day that will dissolve the world into burning coals ... My prayers are not worthy, but do Thou, Good (God), deal kindly lest I burn in perennial fire.'

Yet armed with his new discovery, Luther saw that he could face such fears like this:

'When the devil throws our sins up to us and declares that we deserve death and hell, we ought to speak thus: "I admit that I deserve death and hell. What of it? Does this mean that I shall be sentenced to eternal damnation? By no means. For I know One who suffered and made satisfaction in my behalf. His name is Jesus Christ, the Son of God. Where he is, there I shall be also."'

And so the horrifying doomsday became for him what he would call 'the most happy Last Day.'

AFTER DARKNESS, LIGHT

Before the Reformation, the city of Geneva in Switzerland had the motto *Post tenebras spero lucem* (After darkness I hope for light). It was a city hoping for light.

Then the happy message of the Reformation swept through. In commemoration, coins were struck with a new and far cheerier motto: *Post tenebras lux* (After darkness, light). The news of God's love, generosity and kindness to failures was like light in their darkness. So now, they declared, they had found what once they had hoped for.

Transformed
lives,

TRANS

WORLD

SFORMED

CHAPTER 6

THROUGH THE REFORMATION, A TIDAL WAVE OF SOCIAL IMPROVEMENT WAS UNLEASHED.

Luther had joined a monastery to do good works for God. But he came to see that it is not God in heaven who needs our good works, it is people on earth.

Luther therefore encouraged Christians, instead of retreating to monasteries, to go out into the world. Having been loved first by God, they could go out to love and serve others.

The abolitionists

Take, for example, those eighteenth- and nineteenth-century heirs of the Reformation who campaigned for the abolition of the slave trade. Perhaps best known are William Wilberforce and John Newton, the ex-slave-trader and author of the hymn Amazing Grace. 'God Almighty,' wrote Wilberforce, 'has placed before me two great Objects, the Suppression of the Slave Trade and the Reformation of Manners [morals].'

A Briton knows, or if he knows it not,
The Scripture plac'd within his reach, he ought,
That souls have no discriminating hue,
Alike important in their Maker's view;
That none are free from blemish since the fall,
And love divine has paid one price for all.

William Cowper, poet and friend of John Newton

Wilberforce was strongly encouraged in his work against slavery by John Wesley, the evangelist and founder of Methodism, who wrote his last letter to urge Wilberforce on. 'Slave-holding is utterly inconsistent with Mercy', argued Wesley. It is the exact opposite of the liberating kindness of God

which had been trumpeted in the Reformation. Wesley therefore fought and prayed for the emancipation of both African bodies and souls:

> 'O burst thou all their chains in sunder, more especially the chains of their sins; Thou Saviour of all, make them free, that they may be free indeed.'

And his prayer was answered: the success of the abolitionists over slavery went hand-in-hand with a dramatic growth in black Christianity.

Shaftesbury

When William Wilberforce died in 1833, his funeral was attended by another heir of the Reformation, Anthony Ashley Cooper. Later titled Lord Shaftesbury, he would become known as 'the great philanthropist'.

Trusting himself to God after reading the same book that had converted Wilberforce to Christianity, he had resolved 'with the help of God' to devote his life 'to pleading the cause of the poor and friendless.'

Which he then did with unstinting energy for over fifty years. Through Parliament, he fought the sale of girls into prostitution, outlawed employing young boys as chimneysweeps, established working hours to end the cruel abuse of poor manual workers, and transformed the previously disgusting conditions of London madhouses. He provided education, food and housing for the poor – and the list could go on for pages.

Having experienced the loving compassion of Christ himself, he wanted to share it. After all, he said, 'these social reforms, so necessary, so indispensable, seem to require as much of God's grace as a change of heart.'

> 'No man, depend on it, can persist from the beginning of his life to the end of it in a course of self-denial, in a course of generosity, in a course of virtue … unless he is drawing from the fountain of our Lord Himself.'
> **Lord Shaftesbury**

The Shaftesbury Memorial in Piccadilly Circus, London, crowned by The Angel of Christian Charity, erected to commemorate the philanthropic works of Lord Shaftesbury.

WORTH DYING FOR

People usually walk right past it, or cycle straight over it. But in the middle of Broad Street, Oxford, lies a little cobblestone cross with a remarkable story.

The cross marks the spot where three Reformers were burned to death for teaching that God forgives not the deserving but those who'll trust him.

On 16 October, 1555, two bishops, Hugh Latimer and Nicholas Ridley, were bound together to a stake and a fire was lit in the sticks at their feet. As Ridley writhed in agony, Latimer shouted through the flames:

'Be of good comfort, Master Ridley, and play the man; we shall this day light such a candle, by God's grace, in England, as I trust shall never be put out.'

Five months later, the Archbishop of Canterbury, Thomas Cranmer, was burned on the same spot. Under extreme duress, Cranmer had actually recanted those beliefs that had led Ridley and Latimer to their deaths. But when the day came for his own execution, he renounced his recantation, saying 'for as much as my hand offended, writing contrary to my heart, my hand shall first be punished there-for.' And so, as the fires were lit, he held out the hand that had signed his recantation so that it might burn first.

Latimer, Ridley and Cranmer were just three of many who died for the message of the Reformation.

And their deaths show two things:

First, just because the message of the Reformation was happy doesn't mean the story of the Reformation was without blot. Down through history, people have always divided over even the best ideas, and used them.

Second, and more importantly, the willingness of those men to die for the message of the Reformation proved something. It was not a message about us doing better; it was a message of God's love worth dying for: 'sinners are attractive because they are loved; they are not loved because they are attractive.'

The next

500 Y

YEARS

CHAPTER 7

BATTLES, KINGS, CONQUESTS AND EMPIRES: ALL GET FORGOTTEN IN TIME.

Good ideas don't.

That's why they'll still be celebrating the Reformation in five hundred years' time, the Reformation wasn't just a moment in history; it was about the recovery of beautiful truths.

Today, we live in an age of extraordinary technological advance. But while technology is doing wonders for our health, work and lifestyle, it is clearly failing to provide us with any deep and lasting satisfaction. Restless, fearful and lonely, ours is a generation self-medicating on the Internet, alcohol and anything to fill the void.

For us today, the Reformation has sparkling good news – news of an enjoyable and satisfying God. A God who lavishes his love on those who have not made themselves attractive to him. A God whose love can liberate the most broken and guilty.

What Martin Luther discovered in the Bible pulled him out of despair and made him feel he had 'entered paradise itself through open gates.' Nothing about that message has changed or lost its power to brighten lives today.

First published in Great Britain in 2017

British Library Cataloguing in Publication Data
A record for this book is available from the British Library

ISBN 978-1-91127-248-9

Edited by
Ben Virgo

Designed by
David Gibson & Laura Smith

Illustration by
Elisa Cunningham

10Publishing
A division of 10ofthose.com

Unit C, Tomlinson Road, Leyland, PR25 2DY, England

Email   info@10ofthose.com
Website   www.10ofthose.com

Christian Heritage London exists in the service of London's churches and guests, drawing attention to the advances of Christianity made in this city and commending the claims of the Christian gospel.

christianheritagelondon.org

desiringGod